28 BOOKS TO $100K

A Guide for Ambitious Authors Who Want
to Skyrocket their Passive Income by
Writing a Book a Month

MICHELLE KULP

ISBN: 978-1-7340538-8-3

This book is designed to provide accurate and authoritative information in regard to the subject matter herein. It is sold with the understanding that the author and publisher is not engaged in rendering legal, accounting, or other professional services. If you require legal advice or other expert assistance, you should seek the services of a competent professional.

While the author has made every effort to provide accurate website addresses and other information at the time of publication, neither the publisher nor the author assumes any responsibility for errors or changes that occur after publication. Further, the publisher does not have any control over and does not assume any responsibility for author or third-party websites or their content.

TABLE OF CONTENTS

FREE GIFT FOR MY READERS

AUTHOR ARCHETYPE ASSESSMENT

BOOK-A-MONTH QUICKSTART KIT

FREE VIDEO TRAINING FROM MICHELLE KULP

I have a special gift for my readers! If you are serious about making a living as a writer, and maybe even writing a book a month so you can retire early…I have created a *Quick-Start Writing Kit* that is yours FREE for a limited time. This kit includes:

- 16 Rapid Writing Secrets
- Bestseller Checklist
- Annual Publishing Chart
- Income Tracker
- Book Creation Outline Template
- Author Archetype Assessment
- Video Training

Sign up NOW to receive your Quick-Start Kit at:
BestsellingAuthorProgram.com/free-module-28-days-to-100k/

Introduction

It's always been my dream to make a living as a full-time writer. Perhaps it's your dream, too.

In 2019, I read a blog post by Written Word Media[1] that said the average self-published author who makes $100K has 28 books published. I immediately thought, "I need to make a $100K with my books! I'm going to write a book a month and create a 6-figure passive income stream SOLELY from my royalties."

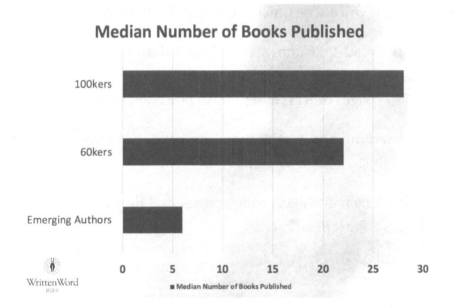

[1]https://www.writtenwordmedia.com/author-income-how-to-make-a-living-from-your-writing/

At the time, I had published eight books since 2011, but most of them were old, the information was outdated, and I had not been marketing them, so they died a slow death.

Starting in 2018, I spent more than a year writing the second edition of my book, "Quit Your Job and Follow Your Dreams." I was earning a few hundred dollars per month from this book but considering the amount of time I invested in writing, editing, publishing, and launching this *one* book, the payoff wasn't huge.

Seth Godin, who has published dozens of business books on sales and marketing, said, "One of my books took more than a year to write, ten hours a day. Another took three weeks. Both sell for the same price. The quicker one outsold the other 20 to 1."

When I read that quote, I realized I didn't need to spend months or years working on one book. I needed to write short books (100 pages or less) and publish one book per month.

Since writing and teaching are my passion, I knew I could easily do this!

My books, on average, are 100 pages, and they fit nicely into Amazon's "Short Reads" category.

‹ Kindle Store

Kindle Short Reads

15 minutes (1-11 pages)

30 minutes (12-21 pages)

45 minutes (22-32 pages)

One hour (33-43 pages)

90 minutes (44-64 pages)

Two hours or more (65-100 pages)

I have focused mainly on nonfiction books.

I'm happy to tell you that after 12 consecutive months of writing a book a month, I was able to create $3,300 in monthly royalties!

When I first publish a book, it brings in about $200-$300+ per month in royalties, and that amount increases over time and with each new book I publish.

I heard another author say, "Nothing sells your first book better than your second book." I've also found this to be true. In each new book I release, I include references to my previously published titles, which creates new readers for those books.

As I am writing these words now, I currently have 11 books on the Amazon Best Sellers list in the "Women & Business" category! My goal is to dominate this category (and other categories):

Here are some screenshots of those 11 books:

Amazon Best Sellers
Our most popular products based on sales. Updated hourly.

Best Sellers in Women & Business

Top 100 Paid   Top 100 Free

#51
Self-Help for Women: 4 Books in 1...
- Ada Moss
★★★★★ 11
Kindle Edition
$9.95

#52
Blowing My Way to the Top: How to Breas...
- Jen Atkin
★★★★★ 497
Kindle Edition
$12.99

#53
belonging: The Key to Transforming and...
- Sue Unerman
★★★★★ 34
Kindle Edition
$12.60

#54
Real Estate Millionaire Secrets: The Real...
- Noelle Randall
★★★★★ 23
Kindle Edition
$4.99

#55
The Memo: What Women of Color Need to...
- Minda Harts
★★★★★ 1,201
Kindle Edition
$13.99

#56
Rewire for Wealth: Three Steps Any Woman...
- Barbara Huson
★★★★★ 23
Kindle Edition
$17.85

#57
Believe Bigger: Discover the Path to Your Life...
- Marshawn Evans Daniels
★★★★★ 1,567
Kindle Edition
$12.99

#58
The Upbeat, Organized Home Office: Five...
- Stacey J. Crew
★★★★★ 94
Kindle Edition
$5.99

#59
Stop Living Paycheck to Paycheck: The Roadm...
- Michelle Kulp
★★★★★ 14
Kindle Edition
$3.99

#60
Why They Stay: Sex Scandals, Deals, and...
- Anne Michaud
★★★★★ 28
Kindle Edition
$3.99

#61
Make Money While You Sleep: Use the...
- Michelle Kulp
★★★★★ 21
Kindle Edition
$4.99

#62
Do Less: A Revolutionary Approach to Time...
- Kate Northrup
★★★★★ 580
Kindle Edition
$8.99

New Releases
in Women & Business

#63
Writing and Releasing Rapidly Endors...
- Elana M. Johnson
★★★★★ 130
$4.99

#64
Quit Your Job and Follow Your Dreams: A 12...
- Michelle Kulp
★★★★★ 34
Kindle Edition
$4.99

#65
Do It Scared: Finding the Courage to Face...
- Ruth Soukup
★★★★★ 581
Kindle Edition
$9.99

#66
The Secret Thoughts of Successful Women...
- Valerie Young Ed.D
★★★★★ 316
Kindle Edition
$9.99

#67
The Most Powerful Woman in the Room is...
- Lydia Fenet
★★★★★ 411
Kindle Edition
$12.99

#68
B*tch Don't Kill My Vibe: How To Stop...
- Renae Owen
★★★★★ 86
Kindle Edition
$4.95

#69
Wealth Unbroken: Growing Wealth...
- Rebecca Walser
★★★★★ 198
Kindle Edition
$4.99

#70
How To Get Anything You Want: A Goal...
- Thea Amrthraa Messan
★★★★★ 108
Kindle Edition
$4.99

#71
Investing in Rental Properties for Beginners...
- Lisa Phillips
★★★★★ 374
Kindle Edition
$4.99

#72
Chillpreneur: The New Rules for Creating...
- Denise Duffield Thomas
★★★★★ 381
Kindle Edition
$9.99

#73
The Brilliant Businesswomen, Your Guide to...
- Danielle Witmeyer
★★★★★ 27
Kindle Edition
$4.99

#74
Amsterdam Exposed: An American's Journey...
- David Wienir
★★★★★ 138
Kindle Edition
$2.99

#81
Passion & Profit Series: Books 1-4: How to...
- Michelle Kulp
★★★★★ 5
Kindle Edition
$8.99

#82
The Fifth Trimester: The Working Mom's...
- Lauren Smith Brody
★★★★★ 362
Kindle Edition
$11.99

#83
Getting Noticed: A No-Nonsense Guide to...
- Lindsay Teague Moreno
★★★★★ 682
Kindle Edition
$9.99

#84
Make It Happen
- Kajsa Crescent Cherry
★★★★★ 3
Kindle Edition
$6.99

#85
How NOT To Write A Book: 12 Things You...
- Michelle Kulp
★★★★★ 19
Kindle Edition
$4.99

#86
Thinking Like a Boss: Uncover and Overcome...
- Kate Crocco
★★★★★ 191
Kindle Edition
$1.99

#87
FORGIVE: Seven Steps to Finding Forgiveness...
- Dr. Charlotte Manning
★★★★★ 11
Kindle Edition
$2.99

#88
Business Breakthrough: Your Creative Value...
- Gail Doby
★★★★★ 11
Kindle Edition
$0.99

#89
Use Your Assets - A Beginner's Book on...
- Alexandria Wolff
★★★★★
Kindle Edition
$0.99

#90
Teach Your Expertise: How to Grow a...
- Aima Vincent
★★★★★ 46
Kindle Edition
$2.99

#91
Stop Chasing Start Attracting: Discover The...
- Kristen Booths
★★★★★ 45
Kindle Edition
$9.99

#92
SEO - The Savvy Way to Ranking #1 in...
- Gurpal Kahlonta
★★★★★ 112
Kindle Edition
$5.99

Volume Boosts Visibility!

I write books mainly in the business genre – books for entrepreneurs and authors; I've also written a few self-help books for women. We'll talk more about whether you should write in one genre only or diversify.

I decided to write this book for ambitious authors and entrepreneurs who have a desire to write quality books that serve readers AND want to earn a full-time income with their books. That is my goal as well.

Since January 2013, I have helped over 250 authors become #1 bestselling authors in my done-for-you program, www.BestSellingAuthorProgram.com.

Many of my business authors are making six or seven figures from speaking, coaching, consulting, etc. as a result of publishing books.

However, I do not have any students making six figures from publishing *just one book.*

If you're a business owner or an entrepreneur, it's smart to write a book that creates back-end income in the 6- to 7-figure range. I've used this strategy myself. I wrote an entire book about how to build the profit into your book first, before you write it. That book is: "Backwards Book Launch: Reverse Engineer Your Book and Unlock Its Hidden 6-Figure Potential."

Writing one book is great IF you have a plan to monetize that book (which is what I teach my clients). However, if you want to make passive income SOLELY from royalties, then *writing a book a month* can help you reach that goal if you're committed to doing the work.

You're probably thinking *"Michelle, this plan sounds like I would need to invest a lot of time in order to reach $100K a year."*

Yes, that's true. It will take you two years and four months to have 28 books published if you publish one book per month. However, I learned from my good friend, multiple bestselling author Marc Reklau (who just this month earned over $20K from royalties on his books), that you don't need 28 individual books published on Amazon; you just need 28 "products" on Amazon. A product can be an audio book, or a box set in which you bundle two or more titles together and sell them as one product for a higher price. In addition to creating box sets from his books in the same genre, Marc also creates audio books to sell as a separate product. He also sells his books in other countries and in other languages on the Amazon platform.

BAM!

I'm writing a book a month and in this month's book, I'm sharing with you the process I have developed, what I've learned, and best practices.

When I tell my clients and other entrepreneurs that *I'm writing a book a month*, I get responses like, "I want to do that!", "Can you teach me how?", "Sign me up!" Because of the positive response, I have created an online course to go along with my **Book-A-Month** (BAM) system which also includes the training, templates, and checklists.

"28 Books to $100K" is for anyone who loves writing and wants to make a living as a writer. I know some authors who would love to quit their full-time jobs, which is a great motivator!

I can't guarantee your results because there are many variables. But I believe if you write a quality book each month on a topic that is in demand and you are consistent with your writing and publishing, then you will have success. I've set income goals for myself from writing a book a month, and so far I have reached those goals each month. I'll share my results with you soon.

Determine your goals and start there. Maybe you just want to write enough books to pay your cable bill, or maybe your mortgage payment or even ALL of your living expenses. The sky is the limit if you're willing to work for it!

Whatever your personal goal is… I believe that writing a quality "Book a Month" can help you increase your passive income and achieve your goals.

There's a lot to learn, so let's get started…

Chapter 1

Why Shorter is Better

"One of my books took more than a year to write, ten hours a day. Another took three weeks. Both sell for the same price. The quicker one outsold the other 20 to 1.

A $200 bottle of wine costs almost exactly as much to make as a $35 bottle of wine.

The cost of something is largely irrelevant, people are paying attention to its value.

Your customers don't care what it took for you to make something. They care about what it does for them."

~Seth Godin, Multiple Bestselling Business Author

In the past, big publishing houses could charge more for longer books. There was also a high demand from consumers who wanted to read longer books.

However, times have changed, and people now have less time and decreased attention spans.

Readers want short books!

Top 10 Reasons To Write Short Reads Books

1. Time and attention are in short supply, so there is a greater demand from readers for quick reads.

2. Writing short books focused on one topic is easier than writing a long book with multiple topics.

3. Fewer words require less time to write (it took me three days to write the bulk of this book.)

4. Volume Boosts Your Visibility (especially on Amazon). You can attract repeat readers who will follow you.

5. Short books involve less risk. Because you are not investing a considerable amount of time or money in creating these books, less than expected sales will not greatly impact you. In fact, you will learn what works and what doesn't work and then use that knowledge when writing more books.

6. You can create a series of short books that explore your favorite subjects in greater depth than you could do in a single, larger book.

7. In this article[2], much of the data shows that people do not finish reading books. Since shorter books require less time to read, there is a greater chance people will actually read your entire book.

---

[2] https://www.theifod.com/how-many-people-finish-books/

8. Amazon has a specific category for these books called "Short Reads." You can't select this category when publishing on KDP, but if the number of pages in your book matches the criteria in that Short Reads category, Amazon will include your book in that category giving it more exposure.

9. You can set a lower price your eBook and get a higher quantity of sales.

10. You can *niche and grow rich* by writing short books in very narrow categories and do extremely well.

I love writing shorter books!

I spent a year writing the second edition of my book, "Quit Your Job and Follow Your Dreams," which ended up being 250 pages!

When I decided to do this "book a month" experiment, I wrote "How to Find Your Passion: 23 Questions that Can Change Your Entire Life" in about three weeks. I published it within 30 days, and right now, this is my top income generating book. It outsells "Quit Your Job and Follow Your Dreams" 10 to 1. I believe it's because people want shorter books with action items they can use to get quick results.

Of course, some books will do better than others. You never know what topic will appeal best to readers. The market decides what they like and don't like. All you can do is write the best book possible, do your research, launch like a pro, and then move on to the next one.

We live in a high-tech, fast-paced world. Most of us are extremely distracted and our time is fragmented. Gone are the days when people buy a manifesto type book and block out their entire weekend to leisurely read.

These days, our time is broken up into short and often disjointed periods. We face constant interruptions from emails, texts, phone calls, Facebook, Twitter, Instagram, and more.

Consequently, attention spans have diminished. The desire to learn new things still exists but most people want to learn faster.

Consider this when writing books. Instead of writing a book on the A-Z of Marketing, write a series of short books that each focus on one narrow topic. For example, the series could include books on these topics:

- Writing Persuasive Sales copy
- Creating Facebook Ads
- Building a Profitable Blog
- How to Create a Webinar

Think micro-topics instead of macro-topics.

6 Types of Easy-to-Write Short Books

1. List or tip book
2. Step-by-step guide
3. Q&A interview focused on a specific topic

4. Single-question deep dive

5. Collection book (for example, top strategies, top recipes, or top performers in an industry)

6. Extended blog post – if you have a popular blog post, expand on it and publish it as a short book

Return on Investment (ROI)

I've written long books and short books, and shorter books provide a better return on investment in my opinion.

I believe writing shorter books saves you time while increasing your revenue. For example, let's say you spend one full year writing a book (like I and many of my clients have done), and you earn $200 a month from that one book. If you were writing a book a month, you could have written 12 books, each earning $200 a month, and your income would be $2,400 per month or more instead of $200 per month!

BAM!

Moreover, you are more likely to finish writing and publish a shorter book because writing a large book that is 50,000 to 100,000 words can be a daunting task.

I work with clients who have spent years working on their "one book."

I encourage you to write short books. You can write the book in about two weeks and the editing process will be much shorter.

When I send my final manuscript to my editor (I recommend always using a professional editor), she reviews it and sends it back to me with changes marked in the document. I review her suggested changes and accept or reject them. Then, I wait a day or two and read the book word for word (which is easy to do with a short book), and I always find a few typos and some changes I want to make.

A 250+ page book would require too much time to write, edit, and review, and I would not be able to publish a book a month with that many pages.

So, keep it short and save yourself the overwhelm! Readers want short books!

Chapter 2

Titles, Titles, Everywhere

If you are going to write a book a month, I suggest you have a designated notebook labeled, "Titles" or create a document on your *Notes* app on your smartphone or computer and keep adding to it. Just about every day, I read or hear something, and I think, "OMG, what a great title!"

Authors cannot copyright a title. So, the title for your book can be the same as another book that has been previously published. However, I would encourage you to slightly change the title and not copy a great title word-for-word.

For example, several writers contributed to a multi-author book called "Write and Grow Rich" which is similar to the classic book "Think and Grow Rich" by Napoleon Hill.

I talk more about different ways to come up with titles in the *Bestseller Checklist* chapter, but here are 50 fill-in-the-blank templates you can use as a launching point to create your amazing book titles!

Numbers Titles

1. [Number] Secrets to [do anything you're an expert at teaching]

2. [Number] Best Ways to Get Your [Book/Product] Done Fast

3. [Number] Strategies for More Productive [Activity]

4. [Number] Ways to [Result]

5. [Number] Quick & Clever [Subject you're an expert at] Techniques

6. [Number] Ways to [Boost/Enhance] Your [Career/ Weight Loss/Dating Options] in [Number] Minutes a Day

7. [Number] Best [Resource(s)] for [Target Audience]

8. [Number] Steps to Better [Writing/Weddings/ Activity]

9. [Number] Secrets of Super Simple [Activity]

10. [Number] Best [Subject you're an expert at] Tricks You Haven't Tried

11. [Number] Unforgettable [People/Places/Subject]

12. [Number] Secrets to [Staying Slim/Making Money]

13. [Number] [Delicious/Trendy/Fast/Adjective] [Noun] You Will Love

14. [Number] Strategies to [do anything you're an expert at teaching]

15. Your Way to Real [Wealth/Health/Prestige/Result]

16. [Number] Tough [Subject you're an expert at] Questions and the Right Answers

17. The Mistake that Will Cost You [Number] [Dollars/Hours/Measurable cost]

How-to Titles

1. How [Current Event News] is/are Changing the [Economy/Industry]

2. The Best Way to [do anything you're an expert at teaching]

3. Your Guide to [Opportunities/to do anything you're an expert at teaching] that Pay(s) Off BIG

4. How to Win Free [Resource/Prize] to [Result]

5. Put Your Skills to Work to [Support/Follow/Achieve] Your [Dream, Goal, Plan]

6. How to Get a Dream [Career] [subject you're an expert at] Made Simple

7. How to Win at [Activity/Career]

8. [Subject you're an expert at] Made Easy

9. [Subject you're an expert at] in [Number] Simple Steps

10. How to Spot Bad [Subject you're an expert at] Advice

11. How to Cut Your Risk of [Problem]

12. Your Final Solution to [Problem]

13. More [Result], Less [Problem]—Here's How

14. How to [Result] and Not Get Burned

15. Easy [Subject you're an expert at] Secrets

16. Why You Shouldn't Ignore [Problem]

Benefit-Driven Titles

1. What Every [Writer/Plumber/Occupation] Needs to Know About [Your Expertise]

2. Why Someone Else's [Product] Could be Your [Chance/Result]

3. Save Hundreds of Dollars on [Activity/Item]

4. Avoid [Mistake]

5. Prevent [Consequence] by [Your Solution]

6. Celebrate [Result] through [Problem]

7. Stop [Mistake] Here's Why

8. Your Perfect [Result] Starts Now

9. Have More [Result]

10. Top Secret: How You Can Achieve [Result]

11. Got [Problem]? Here's How to [Result]

12. The [Result] You Can Get at [Home/Work/Place]

13. Supersize Your [Result]

14. Secrets of [Benefit Adjective] People

15. Smart People [Result]

16. Low [Risk/Cost/Problem], Big Results

17. A Surprisingly Simple Cure for [Problem]

These fill-in-the-blank templates will make it much easier for you to come up with titles.

PRO TIP: Use this same method for your chapter titles. Don't give away the whole book in your table of contents. You want to evoke curiosity, so people actually purchase your book. Create intriguing chapter titles that make people want to buy the book to learn more.

If you get stuck, look at titles on the bestsellers list in your genre for more ideas.

Looking at books that are successful and doing well will inspire and motivate you!

I use a program called "KDSpy" that allows me to see how many copies of a book are sold per month. This is invaluable information when you're deciding which books you want to write each month. When you see a successful book on Amazon, the next step would be to read the reviews and think about how you can write a better, different, or improved book.

It's important that you keep writing your book each month and stay on your timeline, even if you are not 100% sure what the final title will be. Just use a "working title" that can be changed when you're done writing.

Many times, I create the subtitle after I write a book because you learn things as you're writing, and the writing informs the title as well as the subtitle.

Use the fill-in-the-blank template below to plan out your 12-month book writing plan and get started now. Action is everything.

You can get my templates here:

BestSellingAuthorProgram.com/free-module-28-days-to-100k/

Book-A-Month (BAM)
Annual Publishing Chart

Title/ Subtitle	Genre/ Series	Outline/ Write	Edited	Cover Design	Proofed	Formatted	Book Description	ISBN	Pub. Date	Launch Date

Chapter 3

Rapid Writing Secrets

Let's face it, getting started writing while staring at a blank page is hard. You either have too many ideas or not enough ideas. I know; I've been there. That's why I created "**16 Rapid Writing Secrets**" to help you get the book out of your head and onto the paper as quickly as possible.

Since our goal is to write books that will be placed in the Short Reads category on Amazon, we can publish a book that has as few as 11 pages (which is crazy) and as many as 99 pages.

Don't be concerned about the number of pages if it is low. People will want to read your book if they feel it will solve their problems. And the faster they learn how to solve the problem, the better.

I buy a lot of Kindle books and there is something very satisfying about watching the percentage of "pages read" increase on my Kindle app as I flip through the eBook. I love buying Short Reads and finishing the book in 1-2 days.

There is a large audience for shorter books, and your monthly books will fit nicely into this Short Reads category.

I have a developed *16 Rapid Writing Secrets* for you. Here are my 4 favorite:

1. Start with a powerful quote
2. Write the first paragraph
3. Write it out of sequence
4. Write your book on Post-it Notes

I can honestly say that without these *Rapid Writing Secrets,* I probably wouldn't be able to write a book a month. I love writing out of sequence because it doesn't engage my left brain that wants to put everything in a logical order. I do that AFTER I write the book.

So, let's take a look at ALL of the *16 Rapid Writing Secrets* so you can get this knowledge out of your head and onto the paper:

16 RAPID WRITING SECRETS

1. SPEAK YOUR BOOK

Many of my clients do NOT like to sit down and write. So, I have them record what they want to include in their book and then have the recordings transcribed. An editor or assistant puts all the recordings in cohesive order and creates the book. You can do this yourself by downloading the "Rev" app to your smartphone. Then, create recordings for your book and have them transcribed. This is a very quick way to get your book done!

2. HAVE SOMEONE INTERVIEW YOU

Have someone who isn't familiar with your topic interview you about it. Come up with questions for them to ask you and record the answers and then have them transcribed.

3. WRITE THE FIRST PARAGRAPH

When writing a book, the hardest part is writing the first paragraph. Once it's written, though, the rest will flow. You can even write the first paragraph for each chapter and then go back and add the remaining content. Also, you don't have to write the chapters in the order they will appear in the book. Start with the chapters that you feel the most energy around.

4. WRITE THE CHAPTER SUMMARY FIRST

Many books write themselves once you start writing, so creating a chapter summary will help get the ideas out of your head and give you a place to start.

5. WRITE IN A FRESH ENVIRONMENT

Because of distractions at home, you might get more writing done away from your home office. Go to a coffee shop, your local bookstore, or sit outside, anywhere that you won't be distracted from writing.

6. WRITE IT OUT OF SEQUENCE

Many writers get too focused on the sequence of the chapters and never write anything. That's why you need an editor who will review your book and move things around if they seem out of sequence. Or you can move the chapters around yourself once you've written them all. Don't be too concerned about the order of the chapters because the main goal is to get it out of your head. For me, trying to figure out the sequence as I'm writing slows me down tremendously. Just knowing I can rearrange the chapters when I'm done allows my writing to flow with ease!

7. WRITE WHERE THE EMOTION IS

You should write about a topic you have strong emotion around because it is important to connect with your readers' emotions. Write down ideas that are high on your emotional scale. You've probably heard the saying, "Make Your Mess Your Message." What messes can you write about?

8. WRITE THE STORIES FIRST, THEN MAKE YOUR POINTS

Everyone loves a good story. People easily remember stories more than a list of facts. There is power in the phrase, "Once upon a time..." So, write your stories first, and then add the points.

Method:

1. Write a Story.
2. Make three points.
3. Rinse and Repeat.

That's it!

9. KEEP AN IDEA OR BRAINSTORMING JOURNAL

Once you decide on the book topic, you'll start getting ideas when you're out walking, showering, drinking a cup of coffee or tea, eating a meal, etc. As these ideas come to you, write them in a journal (let your subconscious write your book for you). When we aren't trying to *chase* ideas, they will often come to us effortlessly.

10. TEXT YOUR BOOK TO YOURSELF OR USE THE NOTES APP

When we text others, we get right to the point. Text your book via the "Notes" app on your smart phone instead of sitting in front of a computer staring at a blank page. Sometimes, we need to trick our brain in order to get things done.

11. WRITE YOUR BOOK WITH POST-IT NOTES

I've used this method and it's amazing. You'll need some Post-it Notes and something to stick them on to like a poster board or a white board. Do a brain dump and write everything you can think of about your topic on each Post-it Note. Then, sort them out and group them together around a theme to create the outline for your book.

12. BLOG YOUR BOOK

I have done a couple of books for clients who collected past blog posts they have written. They edited the blog posts, rearranged them, and sometimes added new content to them. Then they repurposed those blog posts into a brand new book.

13. PODCAST YOUR BOOK

If you have a podcast, transcribe each episode and use it for a book chapter, and voilà, you have a book!

14. POWERPOINT YOUR BOOK

Many people love using PowerPoint to create content, so why not use it to write your book? Create a slide for each topic in your book, then fill it in with more details.

15. START WITH POWERFUL QUOTES

When I see a great quote, I feel inspired. Many books I've read include a powerful quote at the beginning of each chapter. An easy way to get your book started is to collect 10-12 quotes related to your topic and write a chapter based on each of those quotes.

16. WRITE YOUR BOOK WITH BLOCK TIME

We do our best work when we are in a "FLOW" state, which is when we are completely absorbed in the activity at hand (also known as being "in the zone"). To accomplish this:

- Do your highest value work early in the day.

- Set this time aside as your *block time*.

- Don't do any tasks that are distracting beforehand (email, watching the news, scrolling through social media, etc.).

What are your favorite *Rapid Writing Secrets*? Use what works best for you!

Chapter 4

From Mind Dump to Book Outline

After I have a *working title* for my book, I do a four-step mind dump of everything that pops into my mind about this topic.

Step One

Gather your Post-it notes and some colorful sharpies. Once you have an idea about the topic you want to write about and have researched other successful books on that topic, write each idea on a Post-it Note and place them on a large white board.

Step Two

Organize the Post-it Notes into logical groups based on the topic or theme.

Step Three

Remove any that don't fit. Either throw them away or save them to be used in another book. This is the elimination process.

Step Four

Keep removing until you have 4-6 topics for each chapter. Then take those topics and fill out the book creation template shown below to organize writing your book.

Book-A-Month (BAM)
Book Creation Template

Book	Chapter Title	Purpose of Chapter	Subchapter 1	Subchapter 2	Subchapter 3	Subchapter 4	Subchapter 5	Subchapter 6

*I have a second page of this template that has a total of 12 chapters on it. Your book might just be six or eight chapters, and that's okay.

Congratulations! Taking these four steps will save you hours of wasted time!

Remember, the goal is to write books that will be placed in the "Short Reads" category on Amazon which is why I don't recommend having more than 12 chapters. A chapter can be just a few pages. Don't add fluff or meandering stories to your book. Just help your reader get the benefit your book promises.

I made the mistake of not using this template while writing some of my books, and it was much more difficult to get organized. Of course, things change as you begin to write (like chapter titles, etc.), but this template will keep you more laser focused with your book. Having your outline before you write your book, will help you flow through the writing process much quicker.

I want to simplify everything for you so you can reach your goal of writing a book a month. Our minds love to complicate things because our self-saboteur doesn't want us to finish our book. We must move past the *resistance* and get our book out to the world!

If you are feeling resistance, pick up a copy of Steven Pressfield's amazing book, "Turning Pro" or "The War of Art." You'll learn that the resistance is real and that you must be vigilant and fight against it.

PRO TIP: Don't tell any close friends or family members about your book. Don't ask their opinion or seek their advice because that can block you.

The only way you know what readers like is by writing, publishing, and launching your book. I call this the "Launch and Learn" method! Then, you will see what the market says by the number of sales you get.

Now that I have published more than six books using this system, I can see which books are doing well and which ones aren't doing as well. I don't take it personally and neither should you. Books are very subjective. Some people will love your books, and some won't. It's okay. Keep writing.

The more you write, the greater success you will have.

Think about playing the lottery. If you buy one ticket, your chances of winning are slim. If you buy 10, 25, or 100 tickets, then your chances just increased.

You don't know and you can't predict which books you write will do well. The market decides. Just put forth your best effort, follow the bestseller checklist and tips in this book, and see what happens. Remember, this is an experiment, and we are here to learn and see what works, and what doesn't.

Also, you may have more than one version of your book. One of the greatest benefits of self-publishing on Amazon is if you need to go back and fix a typo or add something new to your book, it's very easy to do that.

Chapter 5

Seven Questions to Ask Before You Write Your Book

People buy nonfiction books to find a solution to a problem. If you can write your book to just one person who is your ideal reader, then your book will feel very personal and really get inside the reader's mind. Don't try to write a broad book that will appeal to the masses.

Go broad and go broke, or niche and grow rich!

Books that are selling well are niche books that solve a specific problem.

When deciding on the topic and the title of your book, you must answer these seven questions:

1. Who is your audience?

Think about exactly who would buy your book. If you have a business, you can write this book to your ideal clients. Try to be as specific as possible when deciding who you are writing the book for so you can write the book to one person instead of a large group of people.

2. What Benefits Will People Gain by Reading Your Book?

List all of the benefits the reader will gain by reading your book. Don't be afraid to be bold when writing this list. For example, "The Backwards Book Launch: Reverse Engineer Your Book and Unlock It's HIDDEN 6-Figure Potential" sends the message that authors who read this book will learn how to make a living with their writing and with their books by reverse engineering the process.

3. What pain does your ideal reader have?

Think about the *pain* your reader is experiencing and why they are buying your book. People are not buying their way *into* something as much as they are buying their way *out* of something. What problem is your ideal reader buying their way out of by purchasing your book? Are they broke, sick, looking for a relationship? You must be super clear on how your book helps minimize or eliminate their pain. The biggest areas people seek help in are finances, business, career, health and fitness, and relationships.

4. What title will best speak to your ideal reader?

I recommend you come up with at least 5-10 titles. Then, create a survey using a free service like SurveyMonkey to determine the top two titles. The survey results may give you some insight into your next book or what the subtitle the book can be. Make sure that you survey your ideal reader to get the best results.

5. What benefits or pain points can you use in the title or subtitle?

Sometimes, a title doesn't clearly represent the topic of the book. Make sure the subtitle does! The subtitle should tell readers exactly what they will learn from your book and why they should read it.

6. How can you grab the reader's attention with your title?

Gone are the days where you can be "subtle" when coming up with titles. Don't be boring. Some of the best performing books on the market have outrageous titles! For example: "The Subtle Art of Not Giving a F*ck" by Mark Manson; "Love Yourself Like Your Life Depends On It" (the title isn't so outrageous, but the cover on the book shows a silhouette of a man holding a gun to his head with a red heart on his chest and it definitely grabs people's attention); "You are a Badass" by Jen Sincero; "Unlimited Memory" by Kevin Horsley (big claim). You get the picture. Don't be subtle, shy, or low-key. It's a crowded market and you've got to stand out!

7. What keywords can you use in the title or subtitle?

Having one or two of the top keywords for your niche in your book title or subtitle will help you get more visibility on Amazon.

Great job!

By taking the time to answer these seven questions, you should have more clarity about who your reader is, what problems they have, and what benefits your book provides to solve their problems.

Keywords

Let's talk a little more about keywords because they are critical to the success of your book.

Readers find books on Amazon's crowded platform by searching for keywords that help them find a book that will solve their problem.

For example, my book, "Backwards Book Launch: Reverse Engineer Your Book to Unlock its Hidden 6-figure Potential", is found with the following seven keywords that I selected (this is the maximum number of keywords allowed when publishing on Amazon KDP):

1. Book Launch
2. 6-Figure Author
3. How to Market a Book
4. Multiple Streams of Income
5. Self-Publishing Books
6. How to Make Money Writing
7. How to Make a Living as a Writer

Selecting your keywords (especially if you have not yet written your book) will help you get clear on your audience and how potential readers on Amazon are searching for information on that particular topic.

I see authors guess what keywords are best for their book, and 99% of the time they are wrong.

The best way to find the right keywords is to first do a brain dump about what you *think* the keywords are for your book; then go to Amazon and type those exact keywords you wrote down in the search bar.

If you start typing these keywords in the search bar on Amazon and the list self-populates, then you know others are searching for those keywords too. If nothing pops up based on the keywords you entered, you should not use those keywords when publishing your book.

I use a paid software program called **Publisher Rocket** to significantly reduce the time spent searching for keywords for my books. Of course you can manually search for keywords, but it will take longer.

Doing keyword research first can also give you more ideas about what books to write and what to include in your chapters. You can find keywords from the search bar on Amazon and use those keyword phrases as the "exact" title of your book.

My client, Lisa Phillips, used the exact keyword phrase people were searching for on Amazon with great results. Lisa's book sales average $2k to $4k+ every month since her book was published almost two years ago. The title of her book is "Investing in Rental Properties for Beginners."

We tried to come up with a clever book title for Lisa's book, but we decided to just use the keywords people were searching for on Amazon and that turned out to be a great decision since the book is still selling well! Her book also makes her 6-figures on the back end which is awesome.

Knowing your audience and what they are searching for is critical to your success.

Chapter 6

The Bestseller Checklist

This goal isn't just to quickly write and publish a book; the goal is to put out a *high-quality book* that will be launched to the bestsellers list and remain there for a long time. To help do this, I have created a *Bestseller Checklist* for you.

Here's an overview of the Bestseller Checklist:

- Start with the End
- Pound the Payoff
- The Snowflake Hook
- Attached at the Hip
- Cover Judgement
- Ramp Up Reviews
- The Preview Presell
- The Synopsis Cliffhanger
- Know Your Quick Pitch
- Launch Like a Pro

Each item on the checklist is described below. Think of these items as creating a solid foundation for your book.

START WITH THE END

First, pick your profit path strategy. The four biggest authority profit engines from a bestselling book are:

1. Speaking Engagements

2. High-Ticket Coaching

3. Digital Courses

4. Live Events

Many authors earn 6-7 figures on the backend of their books. Think beyond the book—your book is only the beginning. It's often the first introduction people have of you, and it can easily and effortlessly turn a cold lead into a warm lead. When someone reads your book and needs help implementing the strategies you presented, that's your opportunity to help them while you increase the profits from your book. Win-Win!

POUND THE PAYOFF

What's in it for them? If your book is all about you, readers will quickly lose interest. Make sure your title, subtitle, and especially your book description shows the potential reader the IMMENSE benefits they will receive from reading your book.

THE SNOWFLAKE HOOK

No two snowflakes are the same. You must create a book that has NOT been written before. Here are some ideas (with actual book titles as examples):

- **Change the Perspective**: *Public Speaking for People Who Hate Public Speaking*

- **Shock Factor**: *The Subtle Art of Not Giving a F*ck*

- **Create a New Process/Method/System**: *Habit Stacking: 127 Small Changes to Improve Your Health, Wealth and Happiness*

- **Make the Complicated Simple**: *The Index Card: Why Personal Finance Doesn't Have to Be Complicated*

- **Against the Norm**: *The 30-Hour Day: Develop Achiever's Mindset and Habits*

- **Contrary Messaging** – *The Obstacle is the Way*

- **Solve a Million Dollar Problem**: *Profit First: Transform Your Business from a Cash-Eating Monster to a Money-Making Machine*

- **Mimic the Classics** – *Write and Grow Rich*

A good hook grabs the reader's attention and piques interest! Think outside the box.

ATTACHED AT THE HIP

Authors need to be thinking about lifetime followers, NOT only one-time readers. Offer the reader a high-value lead magnet at the beginning of your book and gain a lifetime follower on your email list. Also, start a Facebook group for your readers and include an invitation to join in your book. Then, you can develop a relationship with them inside your private group! And, if you happen to sell something on the backend, these readers and followers now become clients!

COVER JUDGEMENT

Readers do judge books by their cover, so make sure your cover is professional, appealing, and attractive to your target audience.

- Pay a professional.
- Do a design contest on platforms like 99designs.
- Take polls and surveys.
- Learn what your ideal reader likes.

I have a professional designer for all of my books, and I never skimp in this area.

RAMP UP REVIEWS

Good reviews sell books, bad reviews block sales. Getting reviews isn't easy, so put together a private Facebook group (aka your "Street Team") and gather your fans who will be the first to read your book when it comes out and are willing to write a review.

THE PREVIEW PRESELL

Put your best foot forward. Amazon has a "Look Inside" feature also known as the "preview" that allows people considering purchasing a book to view 10% of the eBook's content. Make it Count! Don't fill it with Acknowledgements or lengthy disclaimers. Move that material to the back of the book. Put your best material in the front of your book! The goal is to get people to click the BUY NOW button.

THE SYNOPSIS CLIFFHANGER

Most book descriptions are poorly written because they contain dry facts and give away the contents of the book. Your book description should pique the readers' curiosity and leave them anxious to learn more. The three parts to a great book description are: 1) Identify the problem; 2) Hint at the possible solutions; 3) State why your book is the solution.

KNOW YOUR QUICK PITCH

"You know how _____ (problem)? Well, my book [shows/helps/does] _____ (solves problem), so they _____(benefit)." Fill in the blanks with your book.

Example: Quick Pitch for the book "How to Make People Like You in 90 Seconds or Less."

Quick Pitch: You know how some people have trouble connecting with others? Well, my book shows you how to do it naturally and easily… so you can be confident and get more out of life.

Knowing your Quick Pitch helps you quickly and easily explain your book to others.

LAUNCH LIKE A PRO

A book launch aims to get to the top of the Bestsellers list and consequently go from being invisible to visible. The bestseller lists are the most searched lists on Amazon which is why they are so important. Once you are on a Bestsellers list, Amazon often promotes your book to its customers! There are several types of launches you can do depending on your goals with your book. For example, you can do free or paid launches, and you can do them for 1-5 days.

****

There you have it! The *Bestseller Checklist* will help you have a well thought-out book instead of a hasty book that doesn't sell. We want long term sales, not just fast, easy sales when we launch.

Chapter 7

Your 12-Month Plan

I'll admit it, I didn't have a plan when I first started writing a book a month. I just wrote the first book and then the second book and then, in the middle of the night, it came to me that I needed to organize the books for the entire year and decide which genres I wanted to write in.

Let's talk about that for a moment.

Should you write all of your books in the same genre or diversify?

Remember, you can experiment so you don't need to be attached to any one method. You can certainly test writing in different genres to see which of your books do best.

That being said, several authors I know who are making six or seven figures tend to write in one specific genre and are well known for that genre.

One example that comes to mind is Steve Scott who writes under the name S.J. Scott as well. Here's Steve's story:

Steve Scott is the author of over 40+ books and is also an online course creator who makes approximately $30-$50k per month in passive income. When he was struggling to make money online, he was promoting a lot of different affiliate programs.

In 2012, he started writing books and self-publishing on Amazon in the "make money online" space but didn't have very much success at first.

It wasn't until he "niched" down and decided to focus on "habits" that his income grew exponentially. He started his website, www.DevelopGoodHabits.com, and that was the best decision he made because he multiplied his audience and his income in a big way!

It wasn't until he had written several books that one of his books, "Habit Stacking," really took off and he started earning thousands of dollars per month. There are two important lessons here: 1) Your writing gets better the more that you write. 2) You never know which book will take off. Therefore, the more you write, the more success you will ultimately have.

Also, I want to say that Steve Scott has co-authored many books with other successful people. By doing this, he piggybacks off of their audience and has new people buying his books. This is a great strategy for you to think about down the road.

Ultimately, picking one niche is a good idea. However, when you're starting out, you may not know which books will do well or which genre you have more energy around or which types of books you love writing. So, you will have to test it out.

If you are not going to write in one genre, then my suggestion is to write a series of books for each genre and not just one book.

Here's how this would look:

- 2 genres with 6 books in each genre for 12 months
- 3 genres with 4 books in each genre for 12 months
- 4 genres with 3 books in each genre for 12 months

When I started thinking about which genre and series of books I wanted to write in, here is what I came up with:

- Business/Entrepreneurship
- Career/Passion/Purpose
- Self-Help/Women
- Books for Authors and Writers

These are the topics I have the most knowledge about and it's where my energy and passions are. I do know that it's much easier to "write what you know." I've tried to write books that required a lot of research, but in the BAM (book a month) system, time is not on your side and you don't have that luxury. So, stick to what you know.

In this chapter, you are going to create your 12-month plan. Before you start planning your titles and books for the year, you must first decide if you want to write in one genre OR you want to mix it up and diversify.

For myself, I like the idea of having four genres and seeing how the books do. Then the following year, I can decide what other books to write based on previous year's results.

So, in which genre(s) do you want to write?

Ideas for Nonfiction Books

Business	Entrepreneurship
Finance	Investing
Women and Business	Marketing
Sales	Accounting
Self Help	Spiritual
Religion	Health
Stress Management	Diets
Weight Loss	Exercise
Nutrition	Sex
Relationships	Marriage
Divorce	Healing
Habits	Travel

Check out the Bestsellers lists and categories on Amazon for more ideas.

Take the time to write out your 12-Month Plan and post it where you can review it daily.

Blank BAM 12-Month Planning Template

Book-A-Month (BAM)
Annual Publishing Chart

Title/ Subtitle	Genre/ Series	Outline/ Write	Edited	Cover Design	Proofed	Formatted	Book Description	ISBN	Pub. Date	Launch Date

Sample BAM 12-Month Planning Template

Book-A-Month (BAM)
Annual Publishing Chart

Title/ Subtitle	Genre/ Series	Outline/ Write	Edited	Cover Design	Proofed	Formatted	Book Description	ISBN	Pub. Date	Launch Date
Quit Your Job & Follow Your Dreams	Biz/Career								Nov. 2019	Jan. 2020
How to Find Your Passion	Biz/Career								Jan. 2020	Feb. 2020
Work From Home & Make 6 Figures	Biz/Career								Feb. 2020	March 2020
Stop Living Paycheck-to-Paycheck	Biz/Money								March 2020	April 2020
Love Yourself Big	Self-Help/ Women								April 2020	May 2020
28 Books to $100K	Biz/Author								May 2020	June 2020
Career Path Rehab	Biz/Career								June 2020	July 2020
Make Money While You Sleep	Biz/Money								July 2020	August 2020
Spandex Habits	Biz/Success								August 2020	Sept. 2020
Digital Retirement	Biz/Money								Sept. 2020	Oct. 2020
Red Dress Energy	Self-Help/ Women								Oct. 2020	Nov. 2020
Secrets of Six Figure Women	Biz/Women								Nov. 2020	Dec. 2020

Remember, nothing is set in stone with this plan.

If I start writing a book and I'm just not "feeling" it, then I'll change directions. Maybe I'll work on one of the other books from my list, or maybe I'll come up with a new idea.

If you get stuck, find some old content that you can repurpose. For years, I created and sold several online courses. One of those courses is, "Make Money While You Sleep," which is about creating online courses – this happens to be an online course I taught and sold years ago that I have now updated and repurposed into a brand new book!

As I mentioned earlier, if you've written some blog posts that can be repurposed into a book, that's a great shortcut as well. The same can be done with podcasts – select your best shows and use each one as a chapter for your book.

Follow your intuition and guidance and then write where your energy is. Of course, you want to balance that out with doing your keyword research and making sure there is a demand for the type of book you are writing. If you skip this step, then you probably won't earn any income from the book because there is simply not a market for it.

In his book, "Write to Market," author Chris Fox says, "There are two methods of writing a book. You can write, then market. Or you can write to market. One has a much, much higher chance of success than the other. The first method is writing whatever pops into your head…most likely it will result in your writing a book that almost no one reads. Harsh, but accurate. Writing to market is picking an under-served genre that you know has a voracious appetite, and then giving that market exactly what it wants."

Chris Fox has written several fiction books, but he also has a series of nonfiction books for authors.

I do believe there is a lot of truth to what he is saying.

When I am "thinking" about a topic for my book, the first thing I do is open *Publisher Rocket* and do my keyword research. If I find that the topic of my book has good "search volume" and good "average monthly earnings," then I will proceed. If the search volume is low and the earnings are low, then I do not proceed.

I'll come up with 5-10 keywords to research and then decide.

Below is an example of the keywords and search volume for my book "How to Find Your Passion" I found using *Publisher Rocket* when I was researching the topic:

Keywords	Searches
How to find the work you love	5,250
How to find your calling in life	1238
How to find your purpose and do what you love	973
How to find your purpose in life	488
How to find your passion	252
Discover your true north	390

Based on those numbers, I felt it was a good topic to write about, and also one for which I have a lot of energy around. It happens to be my top income producing book as well!

Don't just write what pops into your head. Do your research, and then plan out your books for 12 months.

Chapter 8

Self-Publishing 101

This is not a book on all the details of self-publishing like how to format a book, etc. This chapter gives you a general overview of the important steps in the self-publishing process. I use the following Self-Publishing checklist with my clients in my Best-seller program.

You can use this Self-Publishing Checklist to keep you organized and to be successful:

- Finalize your manuscript.

- Have your manuscript edited.

- Review changes with *track changes* enabled in Microsoft Word so you can accept or reject changes.

- Set the manuscript aside for 2-3 days if you have time. Then, read through it again word-for-word to see if anything was missed and fix it. Also, make any last-minute changes.

- Have the manuscript formatted for both an eBook and print book. *My editor is also my formatter, which is super helpful.

- Decide on your title and subtitle. If you are stuck, do a title survey with SurveyMonkey which is a free service.

- Once you have finalized your title, then purchase your ISBN number for the print book (you don't need an ISBN for the eBook). ISBNs cost $125 for one or $299 for a block of ten on Bowker.com. I usually purchase a block of ten since I am writing a book a month, I know I'm going to use them. Make sure you give the ISBN to your editor to be added to your copyright page.

- I created a publishing company for my books, Monarch Crown Publishing, which is part of my business LLC. I register my books under this name because if I want to speak at book festivals or other events, some of those venues don't accept self-published authors; this is sort of a loophole around this rule.

- Get your cover done. You might want to wait until after you finalize the manuscript because the title and/ or subtitle may change. I usually get three mockups done and pick the one I love the most, then finalize. For the eBook, you will use the front cover only. The print cover cannot be finalized until you know the following three things:

  1) The trim size of the book (I usually do 6x9),

  2) Paper color (on Amazon, you can choose between white and cream paper. Each type has a different thickness which will affect the spine of your cover.) I always select white paper for my books.

  3) The page count of your print book.

I also have my designer create 3D cover mockups that I can use for marketing.

- Document your category and keywords research. I create a Word document called "categories and keywords" for each book and list the categories and the seven keywords I selected for that book.

- Use the keywords to create Amazon Ads or share them with someone you hire to create the ads for you.

- When you publish your book, Amazon only allows you to select two categories. Once your book is published, you can submit a support ticket to Amazon's customer service and request your book be included in 6-8 additional categories. If you are having a hard time finding categories, there is a paid software I used called, "Bestseller Ranking Pro."

- Write your book description. If you are not good at writing "sales copy," then you might want to hire a copywriter. Bryan Cohen offers a service where he will write an amazing book description for you. You can find him at: BestPageForward.net/Blurbs

- Have your final book description formatted with html tags for headings, bold and italic text, and bullet lists, so it looks nice on your Amazon book detail page. I use this free service by Dave Chesson through his Kindlepreneur site:

  Kindlepreneur.com/Amazon-Book-Description-Generator

- The book description will also be included on the back cover of your book. I also include an author photo and a short bio.

- Add a call to action at the end of the book description for the Amazon book page. For example, on the Amazon book page for my book, "Stop Living Paycheck to Paycheck," the last paragraph says, "If you're ready to take control of your finances and get prepared for those rainy days, click the BUY NOW button and join Michelle on your journey to Financial Freedom."

- Publish your eBook and print book on Amazon. It doesn't matter which one you do first. I usually set up the eBook first because it takes me more time to get everything ready for the print version. Also, that allows me to start getting the five reviews I need to do a book launch. I talk more about hiring promoters for your launch in the "Launch Like a Pro" Chapter. Just know that most book promoters you hire will NOT accept your book without five, and sometimes ten, reviews.

- Set up your Amazon Author Central page, which is your bio page where you can list all of the books you have published on Amazon. You can also include any editorial reviews you have there.

- Amazon will link your eBook and print versions so they appear on the same page. If the versions are not linked within a few days of publishing, you can email Amazon customer support for help or connect them through Author Central.

- Get your 5-10 reviews.

- Schedule two-day launch dates. I usually select either:

  Tuesday/Wednesday
  Wednesday/Thursday
  Thursday/Friday.

- Hire the book promoters and decide what type of launch you are doing: free or discounted at .99. If you do a free promotion, make sure you set up those dates in your KDP account. (I go over the launch details in the Launch Like a Pro chapter.)

- Set up your social media posts for Facebook, Twitter, LinkedIn, Instagram, etc. to run on those two days. I use Hootsuite which allows me to set up my social media posts in advance.

- On the day of your launch, promote the book in an email to your mailing list if you have one.

- On the day of the launch, you should check the Amazon bestseller lists every few hours and take screen-shots as your book moves up in the rankings.

- Once you reach #1 on the bestsellers list(s), you can add the #1 Amazon bestseller logo to your cover, if desired.

- Create a marketing collage (I use a free software called PicMonkey) using the screen shots from your best seller campaign and share on social media to express how excited you are about your book.

- After the launch, increase the price of the eBook; or if you want, leave it at .99 for one week to see how it maintains on the bestsellers lists.

- Set up Amazon ads for more rocket fuel for your book (more on this in a separate chapter).

- Set up at least two media interviews for more exposure (more on this in a separate chapter).

- Rinse and Repeat!

I know it sounds like a lot, but I do it every month, and after a couple of launches, you'll be a pro, too!

Chapter 9

Launch Like a Pro

I like to break down my book launches into three phases:

1. Pre-Launch
2. Launch
3. Post-Launch

A book launch is simply a designated time period in which you put all of your book marketing efforts to get a lot of sales (or downloads) of your book.

The goal of a book launch is to get the highest number of sales/downloads in the shortest amount of time so your book will hit the bestseller lists. We will talk more about how to consistently stay on bestseller lists, but the first goal is to reach the bestseller lists.

How to "Launch" Your Book...

You can either promote your book for free for two days by signing up for Amazon's KDP select, in which you agree to publish your book exclusively with Amazon for 90 days. In exchange, Amazon will provide you with two promotional tools: *free days* and *countdown days*. For our purposes, we are only focused on free days so you would use the *free days* tool to give your book away for free for two days.

FREE Book Launches

Why give away your book for free?

To get your book in the hands of potentially thousands of people will read your book, write reviews, create buzz, and trigger the Amazon algorithm. I find that most nonfiction books end up on the paid bestsellers list organically after I do a free launch.

Book Launches with Discounted Prices

If you have a large social media following and/or email list, then you do NOT need to do a free launch. Instead, discount your eBook to .99 cents and do a "paid" 1 or 2-day launch. During a paid 1 to 2-day launch, you will sell 50-500+ books. Every book is different so I can't say exactly how many books you will sell. It also depends on if you have a big email lists, how big your social media following is and how many book promoters you hire during your launch.

I want to mention royalties; if you price your eBook between $2.99 and $9.99, then you will earn 70% in royalties. If your eBook is priced under $2.99 or over $9.99, then you will only earn 35% in royalties.

Obviously, you are not making money on a free launch, but your book will have wider exposure and will most likely go to the paid bestsellers list immediately following the free launch and start making paid sales.

Because I have a large email list and following, I do paid launches for all of my books. I set the price for my book to .99

for the launch days, hire paid promoters, and send it out to my email list and post on social media as well. At midnight on the second day of the launch, I set the eBook price to $2.99 and I find that I get a lot of sales after that at the full price making 70% royalties (which is about $2.00 for a $2.99 eBook).

The BIG goal here is to get to as many paid bestsellers lists as you can, because these are the most searched lists on Amazon and that's where your readers can discover YOUR BOOK!

LAUNCH CHECKLIST

PRE-LAUNCH

- Research your keywords and use them in your title, sub-title, and book description; as I talked about previously, keywords are the words people type in the search bar on Amazon to find your book.

- 30 days prior to your launch, start posting updates on social media about your upcoming book to warm up the audience; write a blog post if you have a blog.

- Create 5-10 titles for your book and do a survey using SurveyMonkey to select the best title. If you're not stuck with the title, then you can skip this step.

- Have 2-3 concepts of your book cover made and post them on social media asking friends and followers to vote for their favorite.

- Decide on a FREE gift (lead magnet) to give away with your book to help build your email list. Create a landing page for readers to download or access the free gift.

- Upload your book about 1-2 weeks prior to the launch so you have time to get at least five reviews (the more the better) before you hire the book promoters. I call this a "soft launch." Don't upload your book too far in advance of your launch because you can only get on the Amazon "**Hot New Releases**" list within 30 days of publishing your book.

- Once your book is uploaded and has been reviewed and approved by Amazon, then you can start getting reviews.

- Price your eBook at .99 because it will be easier to get reviews at this price point.

- Reach out to influencers (press, bloggers, or podcasters) and ask them to promote your book during the launch.

- Send a PDF copy of your book to industry influencers for reviews.

- Create a Facebook event and let friends and friends of friends know about your book launch.

- Write emails to be sent out to your subscribers during launch week.

- If you are doing a video trailer (which should include your free dates if yours is a free launch), post it on YouTube two to four weeks before your launch and promote it. If the book will be discounted to .99 for the launch, then include that information in your video trailer.

- Upload your eBook to Amazon KDP and select two DIF-FERENT categories to put your book in when publishing.

- After your eBook is published, do more extensive category research and add 6-8 more categories in which your book can rank high. This is very important because it allows you to diversify your audience and rank #1 on multiple bestsellers lists. You will need to submit a customer support ticket to Amazon to request placement in the additional categories.

- When publishing your book, make sure to use all seven keywords permitted by Amazon based on your research.

- Submit your book to the book promotion sites about two weeks before your promo starts. I usually hire 5-10 promoters for the launch which costs around $200+.

- Note: some promoters only accept promotions for free books, and some only accept paid promotions. Therefore, be aware when hiring promoters and confirm they can do the type of promotion you are looking for. Some of the promoters I use are listed in the Resources section of this book.

- If you are doing press releases, submit your press releases or pay somebody on fiverr.com to submit your press release to some PR sites.

LAUNCH

- If you are doing a free or discounted (paid) launch, keep your book priced at .99 cents.

- If you have a large email list and following, then do a discounted paid launch at .99 for two days.

- Post to social media (Twitter, Facebook, LinkedIn, Instagram, etc.) daily or hourly during the launch. I use Hootsuite and schedule posts with photos of the book, hashtags, and a link to the book on Amazon in advance that go out several times during the launch.

- Email your list on each day of the launch.

- Be sure to thank everyone who shares, reviews, buys, or supports your book in any way.

- Check your rankings on Amazon and take screen shots as your book rises in the Bestsellers List. Be sure to check international Bestsellers lists as well. Create a document that has links to each category your book is placed on. This will save you a lot of time on launch day.

- Amazon only shows three bestseller categories on your product page, but your book will most likely be on 10-20 bestsellers lists if you selected the right categories. Remember you need to look at the subcategory you chose, and then check the main categories as well.

- Create a marketing collage using a free service like PicMonkey and share your bestseller results on social media.

- Do a two-day FREE launch of your book (unless you have a large email list). The free launch will get you more downloads and potentially add more people to your mailing list if you include a free gift offer at the front of your book.

POST LAUNCH

- Continue to market your book once you are a #1 Amazon Bestselling Author; this is not a one-and-done event.

- Immediately set up Amazon Ads after the launch with at least 500 – 1,000 keywords. This is critical to the success of your book once the launch is over.

- Add the bestseller logo to your cover and resubmit to Amazon (it can take 12-48 hours for approval).

- Immediately set up media interviews once you become a bestselling author.

- Ask for more reviews of your book from people who downloaded it for free (especially if you have an email list.)

- If you did the FREE launch, and your book is not at the top of the paid bestsellers list after it is over; do a paid promotion and hire paid promoters to bump your book up even higher on the bestsellers lists.

- Book Bub is great book promotion service for authors; however, you should know that they reject a lot of books. Also, you have to wait 90 days after you do your own launch before you can submit your book to them. They have over 4 million subscribers and can guarantee sales of your book. One of my clients did a Book Bub promotion and had more than 30,000 downloads of her book in 3 days from that one promotion. You have nothing to lose if you try and get a Book Bub promotion for even more exposure and sales!

- If you don't get accepted by Bookbub.com, then try Ereadernewstoday.com or RobinReads.com.

- I recommend hiring promoters every 60-90 days to maintain your position on the bestsellers list.

- Put 3D mockups of your book cover and links to your bestselling book on the home page of your website (if you have one.)

- Add something about your book to your autoresponder series so you are continually marketing your book to your list.

This is the system I teach to my students and use for my own book launches.

I recently did a paid book launch for the book I published last month and priced it at .99. I hit over a dozen bestsellers list and four of those were #1! Today, I had over 200 sales coming off the .99 2-day launch. I increased the price to $2.99 as soon as that 2-day launch was over. Because I have so many books now, I feel that I can still stay on the top of the paid best sellers lists at $2.99. Eventually, I raise the eBook price to $4.99 if the book is staying on the bestseller lists.

However, if you feel like your book rankings dropped suddenly, then leave it at .99 until it stabilizes on the paid bestsellers list and until your Amazon Ads gain traction.

It's very important that you do a book launch.

Don't make the mistake many authors do by thinking after hitting the "publish" button, readers will magically find your book. I can tell you, with 100% certainty, that until I do the launch, I don't see the increase of my monthly sales for that book. The book is basically invisible on Amazon without a best-seller launch.

DO NOT SKIP THIS STEP!

Chapter 10

Extra Rocket Fuel for Your Book

Marc Reklau, who is a friend and fellow author, has written several bestselling books and is ranked in the top 100 of all authors on Amazon; he told me that he is set to make $31k in royalties this month.

Marc is all about Amazon Ads, and that is what he attributes his huge success to. He started out just like you and I are, and he went from earning a few hundred dollars a month to a few thousand a month to $5k, then $10k, then $20k, and now he's on target to do $31K this month! Crazy!

I'm so happy for his success. He is a great motivation to me and my writing business!

You can check out his books on Amazon at www.Amazon.com/Marc-Reklau/e/B00IZALH04/

Most authors unfortunately don't invest in Amazon ads, and, therefore, their books lack sales and visibility.

Writing, publishing, and launching a book is very important. But if you don't add the fuel to the fire with Amazon ads, then your book will eventually lose visibility on Amazon.

In 2015, I tripled my Bestselling Author done-for-you business by creating PAID Facebook ads that went to an automated webinar to generate leads to a strategy session call. I knew nothing about the Facebook ads platform, but I knew I had to learn it if I wanted to grow my business. That is what I did.

I can assure you that Amazon ads is much easier to learn than Facebook ads, and once you get the hang of it, you only need to spend an hour each day or a few hours per week to have great results.

With $31k in royalties, Marc is probably spending $7-$10k in ad spend – but the point is, it takes money to make money.

Most first-time authors can't invest this much money on Amazon ads, but you can get started with campaigns for as little as $5 per day.

I added this chapter not to teach you the exact steps to set up your Amazon ads (because that would be hard to teach in one chapter), but to give you an introduction to Amazon ads.

My advice to you is – don't abandon your baby after you put all the work into writing, editing, formatting, publishing, and launching your book. Set up Amazon ads and get the visibility your book deserves to generate more sales!

MEDIA INTERVIEWS

Media interviews are a great way to get more buyers for your book.

Nancy Hartwell, my first client in 2013, has now done over 600 interviews. She wrote a fiction book, "Harem Slave," which we published and launched in April of 2013. The topic of that book is human sex slave trafficking, and Nancy has become an expert on this topic. Because of all the media interviews, her book has stayed in the top 10 of the bestsellers lists for seven years now! That's incredible!

In fact, the day after one radio interview, Nancy had 700 downloads of her book! Her eBook sells for $5.99 on Amazon and she gets 70% royalty. So, a 1-hour interview generated $2,933 in royalties for Nancy!

Reach out to podcasters and radio show hosts to be an expert guest on their show once you become a #1 bestseller.

My good friend and fellow author, Marc Guberti, who is a marketing genius, has a podcast show called "Breakthrough to Success" where is has interviewed some amazing authors like: Seth Godin, Neil Patel, John Lee Dumas, James Clear, Perry Marshall and more!

I send all of my clients to him once they become a bestseller to apply to be on his Breakthrough Success podcast: https://marcguberti.com/breakthrough-success-podcast/

Marc Guberti is a USA Today and Wall Street Journal bestselling author with over 100,000 students in over 180 countries enrolled in his online courses. He is a serial podcaster and hosts several virtual summits.

His podcasts include: *Breakthrough Success Podcast, Profitable Public Speaking Podcast,* and *Ditch The Job Podcast.*

Marc published more than 25 books before graduating college and believes that age is not a limit to success.

Marc is a master at leveraging podcasts and virtual summits to drive more sales to his books, courses, and coaching. You can visit him at: MarcGuberti.com.

What are you going to do after you launch your book?

Amazon ads and media interviews are the best ways to drive more sales.

Chapter 11

Income Goals and Income Tracking Chart

What are your personal income goals?

I want to make six figures in passive income from my books, and I won't stop till I get there.

You can determine your income goals based on your current needs. As I said in the introduction, maybe you just want enough to make a car payment, cover a few of your living expenses, or pay your rent or mortgage.

I have found that setting small incremental income goals works well and really motivates me each month as I see my income growing!

Here's the template I use, that you can copy and use as well:

Book-A-Month (BAM)
Income Tracking Chart

Month	Book Title	Monthly Income	Date Paid by Amazon	Running Total

I wasn't sure how this would all work, so I decided to set quarterly income goals so I could use the royalties to pay some of my living expenses and bills. The ultimate goal is to make six figures, but I wanted to get quick wins and feel good about all the time and effort I was investing in this project. Each time I hit an income goal, I get super motivated!

Year 1 Income Goals

BAM Income Goals – Michelle Kulp

Goal 1: Make Car Payment with Royalties
– Hit Goal in April 2020 ($392/mo.)

Goal 2: Pay Car Payment, Auto Insurance and Cell Phone
– Hit goal in May 2020 ($664/mo.)

Goal 3: Pay Car Payment, Auto Insurance, Cell Phone, Cable/Internet, and Groceries
– Hit goal in July 2020 ($1400/mo.)

Goal 4: Pay House Payment with Royalties
– Hit goal in September 2020 ($2000/mo.)

Goal 5: Pay all Living Expenses with Royalties - $4000/mo.
– Should hit this goal in Quarter 1 of 2021

I suggest you set quarterly goals instead of monthly goals because there is always a "lag" with your income doing this system.

The reason is twofold:

1. Amazon pays out royalties after 60 days. After you receive the first royalty payment, then royalties are paid every 30 days.

2. When you first publish your book, there is very little income because you have not yet done a book launch or run Amazon ads. Therefore, no one knows about your book and it is basically invisible on Amazon.

Royalty Payment Example:

- Month 1: Write and publish book 1.

- Month 2: Get five reviews for book 1, set up book promoters, change categories, do 2-day launch for book 1. You are also writing and publishing book 2 in month 2.

- Month 3: Get five reviews for book 2, set up book promoters, change categories, do 2-day launch for book 2. You are also writing and publishing book 3 in month 3.

It's important to note that until you do the launch, you won't have much or any income from that book. Most authors don't do launches, don't get on bestsellers lists, don't get visibility on Amazon and, therefore, don't make much money.

It's important to follow my system if you want to be successful and hit your income goals, whatever they may be.

When I was a single mother of three struggling to make ends meet and living paycheck-to-paycheck, a passive income of $500 or $1000 per month would have been life changing! Unfortunately, I was working a 9-5 job in the legal field with a single stream of income. I wish I had known about this system then.

This "write a book a month" system to create passive income can change your life. It doesn't have to be six figures; it can be whatever you want it to be!

As I mentioned in the introduction, in just 12 months I've been able to create over $3,300 a month in income from writing one short book a month! My goal is to hit six figures in the next 12-18 months!

This is incredible to me especially when I think about what I'll be receiving from social security when I'm old enough to collect (10 years from now) after working 17 long years in the legal field as a paralegal; my social security will be somewhere around $2000 per month. I've already exceeded that amount in just 12 months. That's why you need to start now and create your own financial future.

Seeing your royalty payments increase every month will motivate you to keep going. Of course, there is also the internal reward you will have from having more impact in the world with your message and your teachings from your books!

Set your income goals now and don't give up until you hit them!

Chapter 12

The 30-Day Roadmap to Writing a Book a Month

Now that I've given you the tools, software, templates, tracking charts, fill-in-the-blank title generator, checklists, and everything you need to be successful, I want to give you one last thing – the 30-Day Roadmap for writing a book a month.

It's been a trial and error process for me. In the beginning, I didn't have many of the tools, templates, and checklists that I've given you, so I struggled. I saw right away that I needed to be better organized and I developed these out of necessity.

If you take the time to plan out your entire year with the genres and the working title for each month – then on day 1 of each new month, you can start writing that month's book.

So, what is the best way to write? Daily, on weekends, early in the morning, late at night, in blocks of time?

I've tried them all.

I would write every morning when I first woke up until my daughter and 2-year-old granddaughter came to live with me for a while, which changed my "quiet" writing time and schedule.

I find writing a book in 3-7 days works best for me for a few reasons:

1. I easily lose my train of thought. If I write for an hour or two each day, and then don't get back to it for a day or two, I'm completely lost about what I was writing about or where I was heading.

2. Because I run a -6-figure business with multiple programs (www.bestsellingauthorprogram.com), it's hard to balance working with clients every day, taking care of personal things, and writing my book.

3. I like having designated writing days without any client work or tasks so that I can focus solely on my book. I wrote this book in three days. Of course, I did the pre-work, and I used some of my rapid writing secrets that I shared with you earlier. I wrote each chapter and then put them in order after all 12 chapters were written.

PRO TIP: Don't edit when you are in the writing/creating process. That will slow you down significantly. Just get it out of your head and onto the paper. You can clean it up later or have a good editor help you.

Find the writing schedule that works best for you.

I have an amazing client, Dr. Jeffrey Donner, whom I admire a lot. He has a full-time practice as a psychologist and has written six books so far which I've helped him launch to the #1 best sellers list. He writes every evening from 10 pm to 2 am. He also writes a lot while on vacations in Mexico!

That's what works for him.

We are all different and we have different circumstances in our lives, so I don't believe there is a one-size-fits-all method on how to *write a book a month.*

I can get an entire book done when I have uninterrupted time, but that's not always possible for everyone.

In his book, "Deep Work," Cal Newport mentions author Neal Stephenson, who has no email address or contact information on his website. Stephenson said, "If I organize my life in such a way that I get long consecutive uninterrupted time-chunks, I can write novels. [If I instead get interrupted a lot] what replaces it? Instead of a novel that will be around for a long time...there is a bunch of email messages that I have sent out to individual persons."

J.K. Rowling was absent from social media while she wrote the Harry Potter novels.

Woody Allen, who wrote and directed 44 films between 1969 and 2013, never owned a computer. He wrote on a manual type-writer.

Mark Twain wrote much of "The Adventures of Tom Sawyer" in a shed on the property of the Quarry Farm in NY, where he was spending the summer. Twain's study was isolated from the main house, so his family took to blowing a horn to let him know his meals were ready.

Carl Jung built a retreat in the woods he called "The Tower," which was a basic two-story stone house that no one was allowed to enter without his express permission. Jung would rise every day at 7 am and, after breakfast, he would spend two hours of undistracted writing time in his private office. His afternoons consisted of long walks and meditation. Also, there was no electricity in the Tower. Jung retreated to the Tower not to escape his professional life as a psychologist, but to advance it.

We need undistracted time to do our deep work and deep thinking.

Cal Newport talks about the difference between deep work and shallow work, and he defines shallow work as: "Non-cognitively demanding, logistical-style tasks, often performed while distracted. These efforts tend to not create much new value in the world and are easy to replicate."

Conversely, DEEP WORK is: "Professional activities performed in a state of distraction-free concentration that push your cognitive capabilities to their limit. These efforts create new value, improve your skill, and are hard to replicate."

Deep work is a burden to prioritize, but if we want to write high-quality books that can potentially change lives, we need to find and prioritize that time.

Also, we are creating our own economy with our books.

Instead of being dependent on a job, imagine how it would feel if you could make a living with your writing!

I've had to remove a lot of distractions in my life in order to write a book a month.

- Checking email throughout the day – now I only do this twice a day.

- Continually scrolling through my Facebook feed – now I only check it once or twice a day.

- Binge watching TV shows on Netflix.

- Spending time with low-goal or no-goal friends.

What are your go-to distractions that keep you from doing deep work?

- Relationships with a lot of drama

- Reading

- Consuming content (webinars, books, trainings)

- Alcohol and partying

- Emails

- Social media

- Spending time with friends who are not evolving and growing

- Watching sports

- Binge watching shows

- Work-a-holism

- Anything that prevents you from creating art

If you find yourself making excuses that you can't do this because you don't have the time, then start removing some of the above distractions and you will find the time.

If your life depended on writing a book a month, you could do it.

Here's what my 30-day schedule looks like:

Days 1-15

1. Write and organize the book.

2. Wait a few days, then review.

3. Keep Post-it Notes on the project folder when I think of anything to add or remove or notes to send my editor/formatter.

Days 16-23

1. Send the manuscript to editor for initial edits.

2. She returns to me, and I review and accept or reject the changes.

3. The manuscript is sent back to the editor for final formatting.

4. I then read the newly formatted and edited book word-for-word to catch anything we may have missed in the initial review.

5. While she and I are working on the manuscript, my cover designer is working on the cover.

Days 17-30

1. Write the book description, research the keywords and categories, and publish the book.

2. Do a soft launch to get 5-10 reviews.

Following Month

1. Launch the book

2. Start writing the next book.

Closing Thoughts

What are your dreams? Do you dream of being financially independent? Do you dream of being able to pay all of your living expenses from your royalties? Do you dream of having freedom to spend your time how you wish?

Those are my dreams, too, and I support you in your dreams, which is why I have written this book for authors. I believe in authors, and I believe in YOU!

If you want to achieve your dreams, you must plan your time and prioritize your work.

So many times we want the "result," but we don't plan or prioritize our time. This system requires advanced planning and prioritizing in order for it to work.

My goals are not only financial. I also want to help thousands of authors reach their dreams and goals. If I help authors reach their goals, then their books have the power and potential to change someone's life.

Knowing your BIG why will motivate you on those days when you don't *feel* like writing.

What's your BIG why?

- Self-Expression
- Getting Your Message Out to the World

- Leaving a Legacy
- Creating financial independence for yourself and your family
- Being in control of your time
- Doing what you love and getting paid for it

I hope you will join me on this journey to writing a book a month and create more financial freedom in your life so you can achieve all of your audacious dreams!

Several of my clients are doing this process with me and it's working for them as well.

CONECT WITH ME ON FACEBOOK:

Please join our community here:

Facebook.com/groups/28BooksTo100K/

I wish you well on your journey to becoming a successful author, changing the world with your books and living your dreams!

Michelle Kulp

Bonus

Michelle's Private and Vetted Rolodex

It can take years to find great book promoters, formatters, editors, and cover designers. I currently use the following resources for my books, or these have been recommended to me by other authors.

PROMOTERS: PAID VS. FREE

It's important to understand that there are promoters who will only promote your book when it is free (which you can do by signing up for Amazon's Kindle Select program inside your KDP account) and there are other promoters who only do paid (which typically means your book price is reduced to $.99). Last, there are some promoters that do free and paid launches. I just wanted to point this out.

Promoters for FREE Book Launches

- RobinReads.com/genre-divide/
- BookTweeters.com/#home
- eReaderIQ.com/authors/submissions/dds/
- Fiverr.com/bknights
- JamesHMayfield.com/book-promotions/ *only does free
- FreeBooksy.com/freebooksy-feature-pricing/m

Promoters for Books Priced at Least $.99

***Instead of freebooksy, hire bargainbooksy:

- BargainBooksy.com/sell-more-books-2/
- BookSends.com/advertise.php
- eReaderNewsToday.com/bargain-and-free-book-sub-missions/#toggle-id-1 *****must be submitted 10-14 days in advance!

*90 days after you do a #1 book launch, you can apply for a BookBub featured deal:

- BookBub Featured Deal, Price Varies: BookBub.com/partners/pricing

**If you don't get accepted, try running ads on their platform:

- BookBub Ads Anytime, Price Varies: Insights. BookBub.com/introducing-bookbub-ads-promote-any-book-any-time/

BOOK COVER DESIGNERS

- 99designs.com/ebook-cover-design
- 100covers.com
- FosterCovers.com
- GraceMyCanvas.com
- Archangelink.com/book-covers/
- FionaJaydeMedia.com/non-fiction/

- Fiverr.com/designa2z

- Fiverr.com/cal5086

- Fiverr.com/galuhh

- Fiverr.com/lauria

- Fiverr.com/vikiana

- Fiverr.com/germancreative

- My designer is Zeljka: vukojeviczeljka@gmail.com

FORMATTERS

- **Heather Mize at My Book Team**
  heather@MyBookTeam.com

TEMPLATES:

For DIY formatting, you can get some great templates at BookDesignTemplates.com

EDITORS (All editors I have used)

- **Heather Mize** – heather@MyBookTeam.com

- **Lori Duff, Esq** – lori@loriduffwrites.com

- **Pamela Gossiaux** – pam@pamelagossiaux.com

- **Hollace Donner** – Pailmoritz@yahoo.com

PROOFREADER

- Kimberly Marzullo – kimberlymarzullo@icloud.com

GHOSTWRITERS

- **Lori Duff, Esq.** – LoriDuffWrites.com/lori-writes-for-you-expert-ghost-writer/ghost-writing-rates
- **Emily Crookston, Ph.D.** – ThePocketPHD.com

COPYWRITERS

- Rob Schultz – ProfitSeduction.com
- BestPageForward.net/blurbs

ONLINE COURSE PLATFORM

- **I use Thinkific** for my "Client Learning Portal," which is essentially my online course/program/training: http://try.thinkific.com/michellekulp6975

PUBLIC RELATIONS

- **Christina Daves** – www.ChristinaDaves.com

SOFTWARE I USE

- ***Aweber:** http://michellekulp.aweber.com
- ***Bluehost:** http://www.bluehost.com/track/mkulp
- ***Pop-Up domination:** https://app.popupdomination.com/aff/5d4a184df5895d7c596f5242
- ***Publisher Rocket** https://mkulp--rocket.thrivecart.com/publisher-rocket/

- **KDSpy**
  https://mkulp--leadsclick.thrivecart.com/kdspy-v5/
- **Bestseller Ranking Pro:**
  https://mkulp--tckpublishing.thrivecart.com/bestseller-ranking-pro-special-lifetime/
- **Book Report**: https://app.getbookreport.com/
- **HTML Book Description Generator**: https://kindlepreneur.com/amazon-book-description-generator/

BOOK PRINTERS:

- http://www.printopya.com/book

ILLUSTRATORS

- www.Gemini-h.com/illustrations

- www.Instagram.com/art_of_geminih

Note: Some of the links listed above are affiliate links, which means I may receive a commission at no cost to you if you purchase from those link

Made in United States
Troutdale, OR
02/04/2024

17448842R00056